Toby and Trish
and the Amazing Book of
Acts

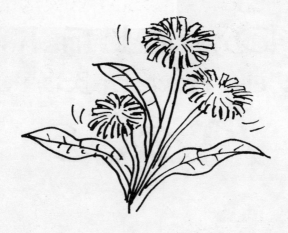

Text copyright © Margaret Withers 1999

Illustrations copyright © Tom Hewitt 1999

The author asserts the moral right to be identified as the author of this work.

Published by **The Bible Reading Fellowship**

Peter's Way, Sandy Lane West

Oxford OX4 5HG

ISBN 1 84101 100 2

First edition 1999

10 9 8 7 6 5 4 3 2 1 0

Acknowledgments

Scripture quotations are taken from the Good News Bible published by The Bible Societies/HarperCollins Publishers Ltd UK © American Bible Society, 1966, 1971, 1976, 1992.

A catalogue record for this book is available from the British Library.

Printed and bound in Great Britain by Caledonian Book Manufacturing International, Glasgow.

Toby and Trish

(and Boomerang)

and the Amazing Book of

Acts

by Margaret Withers

Illustrated by Tom Hewitt

Welcome to the Amazing Book of Acts!

Do you have a friend who is always there for you? The sort of person who goes with you on adventures, who writes down the notes when you are planning a piece of school work, who is there to help you when things go wrong?

Luke was like that. He was close friends with Peter and Paul and learned about Jesus from them. He was a doctor and also a writer and poet, but he gave up all of this to accompany his friend Paul on many of his journeys where he taught about Jesus. He even went with him to places like Ephesus where they were attacked, and when Paul was sent to prison, Luke went with him too. He wrote about Jesus in Luke's Gospel and then told his friend Theophilus about Peter and Paul's many adventures including some when he was there too. So, in the Amazing Book of Acts, we are reading what really happened by someone who actually saw it!

Dear Theophilus
Acts 1:1-5

Dear Theophilus: In my first book I wrote about all the things that Jesus did and taught from the time he began his work until the day he was taken up to heaven. Before he was taken up, he gave instructions by the power of the Holy Spirit to the men he had chosen as his apostles.
(Verses 1–2)

Every Christmas I write a letter to my friends, telling them what my family has done during the past year. Luke is writing his second letter like this to his friend Theophilus. In his first one, he told him about Jesus' life, death and resurrection. We are so lucky that we can read it too in Luke's Gospel.

Now we have part two of the story, which is a sort of diary about the way that Jesus' friends carried on his work. They were ordinary people but Jesus strengthened them with the power of the Holy Spirit to teach and heal people. It is a real adventure story. It has escapes from prison, shipwrecks, friends and enemies. Read a little every day and share in the adventure.

Jesus is taken up into heaven
Acts 1:6-9

He was taken up to heaven…
and a cloud hid him from
their sight. (Verse 9)

When you go back to school each September, you are told that you are going UP to a higher class. This doesn't mean that you go upstairs or even that you have a higher number on the door. 'Going up' means that you have a higher status in the school. Maybe you have bigger tables or can do special jobs or have a different playtime.

…I collected up the books

This is what Luke meant when he said that Jesus was taken UP into heaven. Jesus did not leap up in a sort of magic lift, but he left his life here as an ordinary person and went to live in glory with his Father in heaven. We cannot see him but we know that he is near us always and we can speak to him through our prayers.

I'd like to paint it but it would run!

He'll be back
Acts 1:10–11

'Galileans, why are you standing there looking up at the sky? This Jesus, who was taken from you into heaven, will come back in the same way that you saw him go to heaven.' (Verse 11)

So, there are Jesus' friends standing staring up into the clouds. But God did not leave them for long. Two messengers came to sort them out. 'Don't just stand there,' was their message. 'Jesus has gone to heaven. One day he will come back.'

We cannot see Jesus, for he is in heaven with his Father. If we could see him in all his glory, it would be so wonderful that we could not bear it. Sometimes we get a glimpse of what it is like when we see something beautiful like a rainbow or when we feel God very close to us. It is a bit like seeing the sun through a break in the clouds.

Dear God, thank you that one day Jesus will return and we shall see him as he really is. Amen

The end of Judas
Acts 1:12-20

'The scripture had to come true in which the Holy Spirit, speaking through David, made a prediction about Judas, who was the guide for those who arrested Jesus.'
(Verse 16)

Sometimes we see programmes on television in which a thief has escaped from a house and policemen are chasing after him. He runs down the garden and over the wall, and thinks he is safe. But then, at the end of the road appears another policeman. The thief is trapped. He has no way out.

Judas had got himself trapped. He had been paid to guide the soldiers who arrested Jesus. He saw Jesus dragged off to prison and then crucified. Then Judas realized what a dreadful thing he had done, but it was too late.

Judas used the money to buy a field and there he killed himself. He forgot that, even after sinking as low as he could, he was not beyond God's love and forgiveness.

Matthias gets the job
Acts 1:21-26

Then they drew lots to choose between the two men, and the one chosen was Matthias, who was added to the group of eleven apostles.
(Verse 26)

Have you ever watched a football match in which somebody is badly injured and has to stop playing? On comes the substitute and the team has to continue the game with a new player. Sometimes the match is lost, but sometimes the substitute plays wonderfully well and scores the winning goal.

Choosing Matthias was rather like that. The apostles needed someone to take the place of Judas so that they were a full 'team' of twelve again. Who would be the most suitable? They selected two people. Then they prayed and drew lots (rather like picking a name out of a bag), and Matthias was chosen.

We don't know much about Matthias. One thing we do know is that he witnessed to the risen Christ and, like a football substitute, played as part of a team.

Now there's a thought!

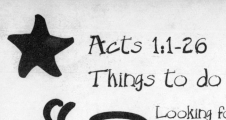

Acts 1:1-26
Things to do

Looking forward

See the world from a different angle—through your own telescope! Using a sheet of thin card, make three tubes of the same length but slightly different diameters, so that the first tube fits inside the second and the second fits inside the third. Put the three tubes together and take a fresh look at the world!

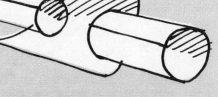

Toby + Trish — Looking forward

I'm looking forward to Christmas...

I'm looking forward to being grown-up...

I'm looking forward to some dog biscuits...

Boomerang loves to feel the wind in his coat!

Whoosh!
Acts 2:1-4

Suddenly there was a noise from the sky which sounded like a strong wind blowing, and it filled the whole house where they were sitting. (Verse 2)

It was a very busy time in Jerusalem and the streets were crowded. It was a bit like a Harvest Thanksgiving at your church or school. Jews from all over the world had come to Jerusalem to thank God for the wheat harvest.

Jesus had promised his friends that the Holy Spirit would give them the power to be his witnesses. They did not know what this meant so they met every day in a house in Jerusalem to pray and wait to see what God wanted them to do. The Holy Spirit came like the sound of a strong wind and flames of fire. The frightened group of friends suddenly found that they had the strength to go into the crowded city and tell everyone about Jesus. If we trust in God, he will give us the strength to do all sorts of things, however difficult.

7

That's me you're talking to!
Acts 2:5-13

When they heard this noise, a large crowd gathered. They were all excited, because each one of them heard the believers speaking in his or her own language. (Verse 6)

I know what Boomerang means when his tail thumps!

I t sounds as if the apostles could suddenly speak in foreign languages! We don't know for sure, but they may have spoken in 'tongues'—strange sounds which many people think is a sign of the Holy Spirit's presence.

Most of the people present would have known Aramaic, the language Jesus and the apostles spoke. Everyone spoke some Greek, the language of the whole known world. But something unusual was happening. It was as if the apostles were speaking to each person in the crowd individually. Suddenly people heard the good news of God's love being told to them in a new and exciting way that they could understand. The Holy Spirit gave Peter and his companions the courage to speak out and their hearers found that they understood them.

Peter's message
Acts 2:14–36

'God has raised this very Jesus from death, and we are all witnesses to this fact.' (Verse 32)

Peter never wasted time. He often acted without thinking. He made mistakes and was sorry afterwards. In fact, he was like lots of other people. Does your teacher ever say, 'Take time to get it right'? Or are you scared to put up your hand in case your answer is wrong?

This time, Peter got it right. He stood up in front of this huge crowd and told them all about Jesus. Not just that Jesus was a good man. Not just that people who did not understand him had killed him. But that God had brought Jesus back to life and that his friends had seen him alive. Jesus was the person whom God had made Lord and Messiah.

Lord Jesus, when we are sure we are right, help us to speak out, just as Peter did. Amen

What shall we do?
Acts 2:37-41

The people said to Peter and the other apostles, 'What shall we do, brothers?' Peter said to them, 'Each one of you must turn away from your sins and be baptized in the name of Jesus Christ, so that your sins will be forgiven; and you will receive God's gift, the Holy Spirit.'
(Verses 37–38)

At home I have got a wooden box with lots of badges in it. There is my Girl Guide badge, my father's Scout badge and the badge from my son's school blazer. Lots of us also wear badges of football teams or clubs. We wear them to show what school or club we belong to or what team we support.

The people who had listened to Peter talking about Jesus wanted to have some sign that they were going to become his followers. So Peter baptized them with water in the name of Jesus Christ. When we are baptized, water is poured over us and we are signed with the sign of the cross. This is our Christian badge. It shows that we belong to Jesus and are part of his family, the Church.

Boomerang's badge says he belongs to us!

14

A wonderful thing happened today—I made friends with Kylie!

The church grows
Acts 2:42-47

They spent their time in learning from the apostles, taking part in the fellowship, and sharing in the fellowship meals and the prayers. Many miracles and wonders were being done through the apostles, and everyone was filled with awe. (Verses 42–43)

Peter and his companions were busy telling crowds of people about Jesus. Many were baptized. What happened to them then? Luke gives us this brief report of what the early Christians were like.

They enjoyed learning. The apostles taught the new Christians about Jesus. They were friendly. People made friends and ate meals together, just like a family. They worshipped God. The new Christians said their prayers together and worshipped in the temple. And wonderful things happened.

This is a good model for anyone who wants to be a follower of Jesus. We can learn about him at home, in church or school. We can share our time and things we enjoy with our friends. We can meet on Sunday to worship God. And God wants us to have happy lives where wonderful things can happen.

Acts 2:1-47
Things to do

Message for the world

Imagine that you are in a strange country and you want to tell people about Jesus. What actions, signs or simple drawings would you use to get your message across?

The lame man is healed
Acts 3:1–10

One day Peter and John went to the temple at three o'clock in the afternoon, the hour for prayer. There at the Beautiful Gate, as it was called, was a man who had been lame all his life. Every day he was carried to the gate to beg for money from the people who were going into the temple... Peter said to him, 'I have no money at all, but I give you what I have: in the name of Jesus Christ of Nazareth I order you to get up and walk!'

(Verses 1–2 and 6)

This poor man sat outside the temple begging for money. Peter offers him the one thing he has really wanted, to be able to walk. But Peter knows that the only authority he has to heal comes from God, so he says, 'In the name of Jesus Christ of Nazareth I order you to get up and walk.'

Maybe you wonder why we don't have miracles like this now. But we do. Our doctors and surgeons give lame people the strength to walk, and they know how to restore sight and hearing. God uses these people to do his work. The doctors perform the operations, but it is God who provides the healing. We can see God's miracles around us every day if we look for them.

12

Peter risks
his life
Acts 4:5-22

Peter, full of the Holy Spirit, answered them, 'Leaders of the people and elders: if we are being questioned today about the good deed done to the lame man and how he was healed, then you should all know, and all the people of Israel should know, that this man stands here before you completely well through the power of the name of Jesus Christ of Nazareth—whom you crucified and whom God raised from the dead.' (Verses 8–10)

Peter and John have been brought before the Sanhedrin, which was the highest Jewish court. Peter, a simple Galilean fisherman, was standing up for Jesus in front of the most powerful and wealthy people in the land. It was the same court that had condemned Jesus to death. When you remember that, you realize that Peter was being very brave—in fact, he was taking his life into his hands.

The court realized that Peter had so many followers that there would be protests if he were put in prison, so they ordered him not to talk about Jesus any more. But Peter refused. He had seen Jesus after his resurrection and he could not stop speaking about it. He was so sure that it was true that he was willing to risk his life for it.

The believers share everything
Acts 4:32-37

The group of believers was one in mind and heart. None of them said that any of their belongings was their own, but they all shared with one another everything they had. (Verse 32)

Red Nose Day has become a special day in Great Britain. It's the day when everyone raises money for *Comic Relief*. Some schools have a collection or a project to raise money in their classes. On television, there is a whole evening of programmes when famous comedians give up time to entertain and raise money for people who are ill or have not got comfortable homes or even enough proper food. And the money comes rolling in.

The early Christians were like this. They really cared about each other. It was unthinkable that anyone could be hungry while another member of the group had great riches, so they shared all that they had.

We're helping people in need

There's got to be something still stuck inside!

14

An awful warning
Acts 5:1-11

There was a man named Ananias, who with his wife Sapphira sold some property that belonged to them. But with his wife's agreement he kept part of the money for himself and handed the rest over to the apostles. Peter said to him, 'Ananias, why did you let Satan take control of you and make you lie to the Holy Spirit by keeping part of the money you received for the property?' (Verses 1-3)

The Junior Church were having a collection for refugees last week. Neil said that his mum gave him £1.00 pocket money so he was putting it all in. 'That's very kind of you, Neil,' said the leader and everyone clapped. Suddenly, James called out, 'Neil's not telling the truth. He gets £5.00 each week.' Neil went red and burst into tears. 'I wanted you to think I was generous but still have some for sweets,' he sobbed. Neil was upset and his friends knew that he could not be trusted.

It was like this for Ananias and Sapphira. They wanted everyone to think that they were sharing all their property, but they were really keeping something back for themselves. Peter guessed that they weren't telling the truth. God knew that they weren't. The shock of being discovered was so great that Ananias and Sapphira died.

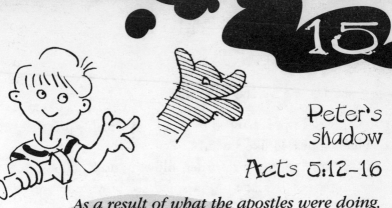

Peter's shadow
Acts 5:12-16

As a result of what the apostles were doing, sick people were carried out into the streets and placed on beds or mats so that at least Peter's shadow might fall on some of them as he passed by. (Verse 15)

Well, it has all been very exciting: thousands of people believing in Jesus, a lame man healed, Peter taking on the great Sanhedrin and a couple of cheats dropping dead. Was it really like this all the time?

Luke brings us down to earth with this little picture of a day in the life of the early Church. The believers met together at the part of the temple called Solomon's Porch. Worshipping God was important. They met in a public place where everyone could see them, so they became well known. They healed people who were ill, and Peter, the frightened fisherman who had said he didn't know Jesus, became a great Christian leader.

As a result the Church grew bigger every day. It wasn't just what the apostles said but the way they behaved that was attractive. Actions speak louder than words!

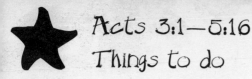

Acts 3:1—5:16
Things to do

Brought to life by the Holy Spirit

The apostles were changed by the Holy Spirit's presence, which appeared like a wind.

Try blowing into a recorder, blowing up a balloon, or blowing across a blade of grass and see how your breath makes the difference.

Blow the grass here...

Toby + Trish — Water music

I'll bring my flower back to life—I'll give it a song...

I should give it a drink!

Through locked doors

Acts 5:17-21

*Then the High Priest and all his companions...
became extremely jealous of the apostles; so they
decided to take action. They arrested the apostles
and put them in the public jail. But that night an
angel of the Lord opened the prison gates, led the
apostles out, and said to them, 'Go and stand
in the temple, and tell the people all about
this new life.' (Verses 17–20)*

Bob was in prison. The cell door opened and in walked a
man in a suit. He said, 'I've come from Jesus. He knows
all about you; he loves you and wants you to change.'
Then the man disappeared. Bob described his visitor as an
angel. 'But,' complained his friend, 'angels wear white and
have wings.' 'Come off it!' retorted Bob. 'I'd have fainted
if that had appeared. God sent an angel who looked like a
prison visitor, because that was the sort of messenger I
would understand.' Bob later became a Christian.

The word 'angel' means a messenger. The angel who
rescued the apostles may have been a mysterious figure in
white or an ordinary person. The truth is that a messenger
from God freed them from prison to continue his work.

Back to the temple!
Acts 5:22–26

Then a man came in and said to them, 'Listen! The men you put in prison are in the temple teaching the people!' So the officer went off with his men and brought the apostles back.
(Verses 25–26a)

Sometimes we see stories about prisoners escaping from jail or the court. We know what trouble it causes and how the prisoner goes into hiding and may never be caught again. Just imagine the fuss when the Council met to judge the apostles and the guards admitted that they had escaped! What happens next shows how brave the apostles were.

They did not go into hiding, but went straight back to the temple and spoke out openly. They knew that they would be arrested again, but they believed that obeying God came before their personal safety. They were witnesses for the risen Christ. A witness is a person who can say, 'It is true because I saw it with my own eyes.' And nothing will stop that person speaking the truth.

Boomerang's eaten Toby's last chocolate!

18

Obeying God
Acts 5:27-32

They brought the apostles in, made them stand before the Council, and the High Priest questioned them. 'We gave you strict orders not to teach in the name of this man,' he said... Peter and the other apostles replied, 'We must obey God, not men.'
(Verses 27–29)

I have a friend called Nellie who lives in the country called Estonia. When Estonia was part of the Soviet Union, it was difficult to be a Christian. It was against the law for Christians to visit people who were ill, collect money, or teach about Jesus. So only a few people attended the churches. Nellie was brought up as a Christian in secret and baptized when she was grown up.

When Estonia became independent, lots of people who used to pray in secret started going to church again. The Christian faith had survived. Just as the apostles obeyed God and insisted on teaching their faith, so had the Christians in Estonia. It is impossible to stop people believing in God, because it is impossible to stop the truth.

Gamaliel's advice
Acts 5:33-39

Do not take any action against these men. Leave them alone! If what they have planned and done is of human origin, it will disappear, but if it comes from God, you cannot possibly defeat them. You could find yourselves fighting against God!
(Verses 38b–39)

At home, I have got some videos of old films which I enjoyed when I was a child. Every so often I watch them again. They are still good, but they look very old-fashioned compared with modern films. As for the cast, most of them are long gone. Other actors have taken their place.

Gamaliel had that sort of thing in mind when he advised the Council not to harm the apostles. They were attracting a lot of attention and their story was convincing. But there had been great movements before which had faded out. Given time, this would do the same. And just suppose that the story of Jesus was true—then the Council would be fighting the work of God!

Dear Lord, help us to remember that the truth will last while everything else disappears. Amen

Punished but happy!
Acts 5:4Ø-42

As the apostles left the Council, they were happy, because God had considered them worthy to suffer disgrace for the sake of Jesus. (Verse 41)

It sounds really crazy to say that the apostles were happy after they had been punished. Did they enjoy being hurt and disgraced? Of course not! The Council's order that the apostles should be whipped gave them two reasons for being happy. First, it gave them an opportunity to show their loyalty to Jesus. Second, it reminded them that Jesus had died for them, but was now alive for ever. Somehow they were sharing in Jesus' cross and one day would share in his glorious new life.

There will be times when it is hard to be a Christian. We should not look for difficulties but, if bad times come, we can remember that Jesus is with us even when things are difficult. We have to try to remember, too, that there are many Christians who suffer *because* they believe in Jesus.

Ouch! My best friend, Kylie, trod on my foot!

Speaking out

Sometimes we have to speak out and disagree when we know that something is wrong. Make a list or draw a picture of things that are right and things that are wrong. What would Jesus want us to do?

RIGHT   WRONG

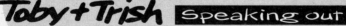

Toby + Trish   Speaking out

You should have told me we were going the wrong way

How (puff) could (gasp) I (puff)?

We can't do everything!
Acts 6:1-4

The twelve apostles called the whole group of believers together and said, 'It is not right for us to neglect the preaching of God's word in order to handle finances.' (Verse 2)

'Why should I have to help wash up?' asked Robert. 'None of my friends do.' Robert's mum had just started working in the local town. She was already doing all of the cooking and washing; now she was earning money so that they could enjoy some extra things like a car and a holiday. She simply did not have time to do all the household chores on her own, so Emma did the dusting and Robert helped to wash up.

You'd think paper plates had never been invented!

It was just the same in the early Church. The apostles were too busy teaching about Jesus to do the other jobs, so they asked for seven helpers to carry out the practical work of distributing money to the poor. This is part of being a family. When one person has too much to do, everyone helps out.

22

My teacher put me in charge of pencils, but they're all blunt!

Seven helpers
Acts 6:5-7

The whole group was pleased with the apostles' proposal, so they chose Stephen, a man full of faith and the Holy Spirit, and Philip, Prochorus, Nicanor, Timon, Parmenas, and Nicolaus... The group presented them to the apostles, who prayed and placed their hands on them. (Verses 5–6)

Where I live, we have just chosen a chairman to look after the roads and gardens. But there is too much for him to do, so we have also chosen someone to sweep the paths, someone to cut the hedges, a treasurer to look after the money and a secretary to write the letters.

The Christians chose seven people to help with the practical jobs. They included Stephen, who was full of faith. They were authorized by the apostles praying and laying their hands on their heads.

It is the same in the Church today. Nobody can say, 'I have decided to be a vicar' or 'I am going to lead a youth club'. They have to be chosen and authorized. Sometimes, this is done by praying and placing hands on the person's head, just as the apostles did.

Stephen is arrested
Acts 6:8-15

'We heard him say that this Jesus of Nazareth will tear down the Temple and change all the customs which have come down to us from Moses!'
(Verse 14)

Cup your hands around your eyes. You cannot see very clearly. Then take them away and look around. You can see much more!

Boomerang can only see this much!

The apostles were all local Jewish men who had known Jesus. The temple was the centre of their worship and they kept the Law of Moses. Stephen and his fellow workers saw things differently. They all spoke Greek and knew more about the outside world. Stephen realized that God was too great to be contained in the temple, and that the gospel, which means the good news of Jesus, was more important than the Law of Moses. The Jewish authorities arrested him because they felt that Stephen was trying to destroy their religion.

Stephen's work was brief but he was the first person to see that the gospel belonged to the whole world.

24

Stephen speaks out
Acts 7:44-53

You are the ones who received God's law, that was handed down by angels—yet you have not obeyed it! (Verse 53)

The Old Testament can be called 'God's story book'. It tells of God's love for his chosen people, Israel. It tells about the great leaders and prophets and how the people of Israel were often disobedient.

Stephen knew his history. He told the Council the story of the Jewish nation, how the people had disobeyed God again and again. Lastly, he told how God had been with their ancestors as they travelled through the desert, and how Solomon had built the temple. 'But,' he finished, 'God does not live in houses. You too have disobeyed God. You persecuted his prophets, and now you have killed his servant, Jesus. You were given God's law and you disobeyed it!'

Stephen was brave. He told people truths that they didn't want to hear, but he was able to show courage because he knew that Jesus was alive.

Stephen is stoned
Acts 7:54—8:1a

Stephen knelt down and cried out in a loud voice, 'Lord! Do not remember this sin against them!' He said this and died. And Saul approved of his murder. (7:60—8:1a)

This was not a trial but murder by an angry mob. When people were stoned, they were taken to a high place and thrown to the ground below. If that didn't kill them, large stones were thrown on top of them. While this was happening, Stephen forgave his murderers, just as Jesus had done when he was crucified.

Christian means 'Little Christ'. It means that we show our faith by copying the way that Jesus lived. It is hard to forgive people who are unkind to us, but, like Stephen, we have to try to follow Jesus' example. Saul saw Stephen die and you will soon read how he never forgot the way that it happened.

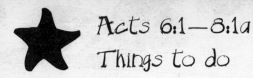

Acts 6:1—8:1a
Things to do

Spread it!

Imagine you told two friends about Jesus on Sunday, and they told two friends each on Monday, and so on. How many people would have heard about Jesus by next Sunday? To work out the answer, take a large sheet of paper and draw a diagram like the one shown. Then count up the people!

Toby + Trish — Paper chase

If you tear a piece of paper in half six times, how many pieces have you got?

I'll tell you in a minute...

ANSWER: 64

Scattered!
Acts 8:1-4

That very day the church in Jerusalem began to suffer cruel persecution. All the believers, except the apostles, were scattered throughout the provinces of Judea and Samaria... The believers who were scattered went everywhere, preaching the message.
(Verses 1b and 4)

My garden is rather neglected and there are several dandelions growing in the grass. Have you ever picked and blown a 'dandelion clock'? You tell the time by counting an hour for each puff it takes to blow away all the fluffy seeds. Then each seed lands somewhere and grows into another dandelion.

Stephen's death aroused a great fury in Saul. He went from house to house arresting the believers and putting them in prison. But a lot of them got away. They escaped from Jerusalem and, just like the dandelion seeds, were scattered far and wide. And so, each believer taught about Jesus to his new neighbours and, just like dandelions, the Church started to grow in other towns and villages besides Jerusalem.

35

27

Philip in Samaria
Acts 8:5-8

I'm going to ask Kylie to come to Sunday school this week ... well, next week, definitely!

Philip went to the principal city in Samaria and preached the Messiah to the people there.
(Verse 5)

When the Christians were scattered abroad, Philip, one of the seven helpers of the apostles, arrived in Samaria. Now, this is remarkable because the Jews would have nothing to do with the Samaritans. The fact that Philip went there was another step towards showing that Jesus was for the whole world, not just a few chosen people.

What happened? Philip told them the story of Jesus. He told them that Jesus was the Christ whom they had been waiting for. Crowds came to listen and people were healed. Everyone in the city was very glad because of what was happening.

Dear God, thank you that the story of Jesus brings happiness and wholeness to everyone who receives it. Amen

Some things cannot be bought
Acts 8:14-25

The apostles in Jerusalem heard that the people of Samaria had received the word of God, so they sent Peter and John to them… Simon (the magician) saw that the Spirit had been given to the believers when the apostles placed their hands on them. So he offered money to Peter and John, and said, 'Give this power to me too, so that anyone I place my hands on will receive the Holy Spirit.'
(Verses 14 and 18–19)

There were lots of fortune tellers and magicians like Simon in Jesus' time, just as astrologers write horoscopes in newspapers today or sell lucky charms and claim to be able to tell your fortune.

Perhaps Simon thought the power of the Holy Spirit was a new trick, so he offered to buy the gift from the apostles.

Peter's answer to Simon is worth remembering. 'You can't buy God's gift with money! Your heart is not right in God's sight.' The gift of the Holy Spirit comes from God. It does not depend on money but on your relationship with God.

Something else you can't buy with money— love!

Philip meets the Ethiopian
Acts 8:26-35

I like to read when I'm in a railway carriage!

Now an Ethiopian eunuch, who was an important official in charge of the treasury of the queen of Ethiopia, was on his way home. He had been to Jerusalem to worship God and was going back home in his carriage. As he rode along, he was reading from the book of the prophet Isaiah. The Holy Spirit said to Philip, 'Go over to that carriage and stay close to it.' (Verses 27–29)

There was a road that went south from Jerusalem through Bethlehem and Hebron to Gaza and eventually to Egypt. It was the road that Mary, Joseph and Jesus would have taken when they escaped from Herod to the safety of Egypt. What had brought this wealthy Ethiopian to travel on it?

Many people had grown tired of worshipping many gods. They were attracted to the Jewish idea of one God and his commandments. They read the scriptures and were called 'God-fearers'. The Ethiopian was one of them. As he returns from worshipping God in the temple, he is reading from the book of Isaiah—and Philip uses the opportunity to teach him about Jesus.

The Ethiopian is baptized
Acts 8:36-40

They came to a place where there was some water, and the official said, 'Here is some water. What is to keep me from being baptized?' (Verse 36)

Do you remember your first day at school? Maybe you had new school uniform—shirt, skirt or trousers and even a tie. Or you may have just put on clean clothes and polished shoes. And, as you walked through the classroom door, you started a new part of your life. You became a member of the school.

When the Ethiopian became a believer, he was baptized. Christians at that time were baptized by being plunged in running water, like a river. It symbolized three things—washing, like your clean clothes; a new life, like your walking through the classroom door; belonging to Christ, like your belonging to your school.

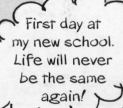

First day at my new school. Life will never be the same again!

The story goes that this man went home rejoicing and took the Christian faith to Ethiopia. Thanks to Philip's teaching, the good news of Jesus arrived in Africa!

Acts 8:1-40
Things to do

Docking procedure

When Philip set out from Samaria, he had no idea he was going to meet up with the Ethiopian. But God knew! Think of an unexpected meeting or conversation you might have had recently. How did you manage to be in the same place at the same time as the person you spoke with?

Saul sees the light
Acts 9:1-6

As Saul was coming near the city of Damascus, suddenly a light from the sky flashed around him... 'I am Jesus, whom you persecute,' the voice said. 'But get up and go into the city, where you will be told what you must do.' (Verses 3 and 5b–6)

Damascus is 140 miles from Jerusalem and Saul would have had to walk. It would have taken about a week. What did he think about? He was full of hate for the Christians but he must also have remembered Stephen's death and how he forgave his murderers. He must have felt very confused.

We do not know whether the light that struck Saul to the ground was lightning or sunstroke. The important thing is that Paul met Jesus and it changed his life. The first thing he had to do was to obey a command. Being a Christian means obeying the commands of Jesus. Saul had been doing what he had thought best; from now on he would do what Jesus wanted. He was a new person.

41

Waiting for instructions
Acts 9:7-9

Saul got up from the ground and opened his eyes, but could not see a thing. So they took him by the hand and led him into Damascus. (Verse 8)

Have you ever thought what it must be like not to be able to see? With a friend, make a simple obstacle course—a couple of stools placed in the living-room will do. Walk through the course, then close your eyes and, *with your friend's help so that you don't hurt yourself*, walk through it again. The first time was easy; how did you feel the second time?

How would you have felt if you had been in a strange place and had not had a friend to help you?

Saul had been a powerful man but it was not until he lost his sight and was helpless that he heard and answered Jesus' call. We sometimes use the words 'blind' or 'in the dark' to describe people who do not want to notice things. Can you think of an example?

33

Brother Toby, can you lend me 20p?

Help on the way
Acts 9:10–19

Ananias went, entered the house where Saul was, and placed his hands on him. 'Brother Saul,' he said, 'the Lord has sent me…' At once something like fish scales fell from Saul's eyes, and he was able to see again. He stood up and was baptized.
(Verses 17a–18)

Scary stuff! God tells Ananias to go to meet Saul, the enemy of the Christians. Imagine how he felt. He could be arrested and might be tortured to give the names of other Christians. But, when Ananias met Saul, none of that fear showed. He called him 'Brother Saul' to show that he trusted him and accepted him as a fellow believer. Belief in Jesus had turned an enemy into a friend. Then Saul started his new life by being baptized.

Baptism is the sign of a person believing in Jesus. It makes the person a member of God's family, the Church. Before a person is baptized, he or she may say, 'I turn to Christ.' You may have been baptized as a baby or you may be looking forward to it when you are older.

43

Saul escapes from Damascus
Acts 9:19-25

After many days had gone by, the Jews met together and made plans to kill Saul, but he was told of their plan... One night Saul's followers took him and let him down through an opening in the wall, lowering him in a basket. (Verses 23 and 25)

How many days does Luke mean by 'many'? Seven, forty, a hundred? A thousand is the nearest answer, for Saul worked and taught about Jesus in Damascus for about three years. He even wrote a letter to his friends in Galatia telling them all about it!

Saul's Christian life began with danger and must have reminded him of Stephen's death. The Jewish authorities were determined to kill him, so they put guards on the city gates to watch for him. The city walls were so thick that they had houses on top whose windows overhung the walls. At the dead of night, Saul was taken to one of these houses, let down the wall in a basket and smuggled out of Damascus. Saul's life of adventure had begun!

Gosh! Friday already. The week has flown!

Kylie and I are going to Sunday school together next week

On to Jerusalem
Acts 9:26–28

Saul went to Jerusalem and tried to join the disciples. But they would not believe that he was a disciple, and they were all afraid of him. Then Barnabas came to his help and took him to the apostles. (Verses 26–27a)

Saul has now met three people who showed him what it was like to be a follower of Jesus. He helped to kill Stephen by looking after the coats of the murderers. But he remembered the way that Stephen died and it helped him towards becoming a Christian. Then there was Ananias, who called Saul 'brother' and baptized him. Now there is Barnabas, who did in Jerusalem what Ananias had done in Damascus. His courage and trust helped Saul to be accepted there.

How did you learn about Jesus? Was it from your mother or father? Maybe it was at school or maybe you have a friend who took you along to church. You are finding out more about him as you read this book. Becoming a follower of Jesus nearly always depends on someone else's example.

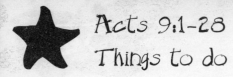

Acts 9:1-28
Things to do

Lighting the way

Which of these items would help someone who couldn't see? Can you think of any other ways to help?

Toby + Trish   See what you mean

It's Saturday—I'm going to keep my eyes shut all morning ...

I'll just see what's for breakfast

Peter in Lydda
Acts 9:32-35

Peter travelled everywhere, and on one occasion he went to visit God's people who lived in Lydda. There he met a man named Aeneas who was paralysed... 'Aeneas,' Peter said to him, 'Jesus Christ makes you well. Get up and make your bed.'
(Verses 32–34)

I hope you have not forgotten Peter. The last time you read about him was when he caught Simon trying to buy the gift of the Holy Spirit. This story really follows that one, but Luke has been telling us about Philip's and then Saul's adventures as they taught people about Jesus.

Here is Peter in action again. But the story shows more than that. It tells us firmly where Peter's power came from. He did not say, 'I can make you well.' He said, 'Jesus Christ makes you well.' Peter never claimed any power of his own but knew that he was only a channel of God's power. We sometimes think just about what we can do, and forget how much more Jesus can do by using us.

Mum says she can only help you to get well if you do as the doctor says

37

Tabitha, get up!
Acts 9:36-42

In Joppa there was a woman named Tabitha, who was a believer... She spent all her time doing good and helping the poor. At that time she became ill and died. (Verses 36–37a)

Imagine the newspaper headline: 'Tabitha comes back to life!' Let's leave what Peter did this time and find out more about the other characters in the story.

> Jesus has no hands but our hands

What are Tabitha and her friends called? They are described as 'believers', but Luke used a Greek word, 'hagios', which can mean 'holy' or 'different' people. Christians are different, not because we are better or more important, but because God has called us to do his work on earth. It was Jesus' power that healed Tabitha, not Peter's. We, too, can be used by Jesus to help those in need.

Thank you, dear God, that you have something for each of us to do, however small it may seem. Amen

Cornelius the Roman soldier
Acts 10:1–8

There was a man in Caesarea named Cornelius,
who was a captain in the Roman regiment called
'The Italian Regiment'. He was a religious man; he
and his whole family worshipped God. He also did
much to help the Jewish poor people and was
constantly praying to God. (Verses 1–2)

A centurian in the Roman army was like a company sergeant-major in our army today. He would have been a good leader, able to fight well and give orders but also take them. Cornelius was the sort of man who knew what courage and loyalty were. He was a God-fearer (remember the Ethiopian who was baptized by Philip?) who had got tired of the Roman faiths and practices and started to worship the true God. He was also a kindly man who helped those who were in need. And he was about to meet Peter...

Perhaps we do not know much about the God to whom we pray, but being aware of his presence can make us close enough to God to hear and respond to his call.

> You look a bit like a Roman soldier!

Peter learns a lesson
Acts 10:9-16

The voice spoke to Peter again, 'Do not consider anything unclean that God has declared clean.' (Verse 15)

Before Peter could meet Cornelius, he had to learn a lesson. He had gone on to the flat roof of the house to pray. Perhaps there was an awning there to keep off the heat of the sun and it wove into a dream. Anyway, a sheet holding animals appeared and a voice told Peter to kill and eat them. Now the Jews had laws that only animals that chewed the cud and had cloven hooves could be eaten. All the others were 'unclean'.

The point of the dream was that it is up to God, not up to us, to judge what (or who) is acceptable. Peter would have called anyone who wasn't Jewish 'unclean' but, in this vision, God prepared him to meet and accept Cornelius, the Roman soldier.

Mum tried to wash this off— but it's the design on the T-shirt!

Peter meets Cornelius

Acts 1Ø:17-33

Peter said to them, 'You yourselves know very well that a Jew is not allowed by his religion to visit or associate with Gentiles. But God has shown me that I must not consider any person ritually unclean or defiled. (Verse 28)

I was teaching a new class on their first day in school. As they sat down, trouble broke out between two girls. 'I'm not to sit next to her,' said Louise. 'No, I won't sit here either!' retorted Sharon. Why had these girls quarrelled? I found that Sharon's grandmother had had a row with Louise's grandmother fifty years ago and the families had been enemies ever since!

There are many reasons why people do not talk to each other. But it is not up to us to decide who is acceptable and who isn't. The Jews would not accept anyone who was not Jewish. They called them 'Gentiles' and would not enter their houses. Peter broke the rules by visiting Cornelius. God was breaking down the barriers between people and he can still do that today.

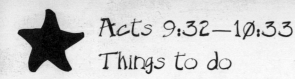

Peter the great!

Imagine you are a newspaper reporter following Peter as he travels around. Which stories would you report and why? Who else would you interview to find out more about Peter? Jot down a list of the people you want to interview and where they live.

Toby + Trish Feet first

The Russian king, Peter the Great, was so big, they put his boots in a museum!

I'd like to see Simon Peter's sandals...

LIFE-SAVING CLASS

I thought learning to swim was enough!

Cornelius starts his Christian journey
Acts 10:38-48

While Peter was still speaking, the Holy Spirit came down on all those who were listening to his message... So he ordered them to be baptized in the name of Jesus Christ. Then they asked him to stay with them for a few days. (Verses 44 and 48)

One exciting thing at the Cup Final happens after the match. Eighty thousand people start singing the hymn, 'Abide with me'. Everyone is caught up in the tide of excitement and companionship. It is the same at any meeting with a great speaker. People can be inspired and changed.

As Peter was speaking, things began to happen. Cornelius and his friends were inspired and began to praise God as he gave them his Holy Spirit. They were baptized immediately. This was a sign that they had been welcomed into the Christian community, the Church. Then Cornelius asked Peter to stay for a few days so that they could learn more about Jesus. It is the same for every Christian. Being baptized and receiving the Holy Spirit is not the end of the story but the beginning.

Great things in Antioch
Acts 11:19-26

Believers who were from Cyprus and Cyrene went to Antioch and proclaimed the message to Gentiles also, telling them the Good News about the Lord Jesus. (Verse 20)

My suitcase was in the attic and I needed it. I stood on the first step of the ladder to open the trap-door. I stood on the second step and I could touch the case with my fingertip. I moved on to the third step and I got my head through the trap-door. I took out the case. Now, I could go on my journey!

Here in Acts, we see the first time that the Gentiles were taught about Jesus. There were three steps on the way. The first step was when Philip preached to the Samaritans who believed in the Jewish God. The second step was when Peter accepted Cornelius, who was a Roman. The third step was when some believers preached to the Gentiles in Antioch. The story of Jesus had started to travel around the whole world.

Three steps to finding Boomerang. You whistle, you shout, then you go and look!

Herod needs friends
Acts 12:1-5

About this time King Herod began to persecute some members of the church. He had James, the brother of John, put to death by the sword. When he saw that this pleased the Jews, he went on to arrest Peter. (Verses 1–3a)

The King Herod about whom Luke is writing was also called Herod Agrippa. He was popular because he kept all of the Jewish laws. Now that many Jews were becoming Christians, Herod felt unsafe. These people could turn against him. Herod decided to make himself more popular with the Jews by arresting the Christians.

He had James, John's brother and one of Jesus' disciples, killed, and Peter put in prison.

Weak leaders often behave like this. They think that some of their people are not satisfied  with them so they do something to make themselves popular, like joining in a war or making new laws. This is bad leadership because it causes harm rather than good to some people and the popularity does not last for long.

Peter is set free
Acts 12:6-11

The night before Herod was going to bring him out to the people, Peter was sleeping between two guards. Suddenly an angel of the Lord stood there, and a light shone in the cell. The angel shook Peter by the shoulder, woke him up, and said, 'Hurry! Get up!' At once the chains fell off Peter's hands. (Verses 6a–7)

Luke was a friend of both Peter and Paul and went on some of their journeys. While they were travelling, they told him about their adventures that you have read about, and he wrote them down later. Imagine how exciting it must have been listening to Peter telling his story of a thrilling rescue and escape from prison. God had acted to rescue Peter from Herod's power.

What does this tell us about God? It does not mean that he will always make things all right like some sort of magician. It shows that, if we trust him, he will rescue us from all sorts of situations so that we can go on doing his work for him.

Knock, knock, who's there?
Acts 12:12-17

Peter knocked at the outside door, and a servant named Rhoda came to answer it. She recognized Peter's voice and was so happy that she ran back in without opening the door. (Verses 13–14a)

There was a knock at my door one Sunday afternoon. I opened it and there was my friend Kirsty, all the way from Australia. 'Well, aren't you going to ask me in?' she laughed while I stood there staring at her. I was so surprised that I did not know what to say or do for a minute!

> It's easier to get out of jail than into this house!

Poor Peter! He escapes from prison and goes straight to a Christian home, only to find that Rhoda leaves him out in the cold. She is too surprised to let him in, but what amazement and questions there must have been when Peter finally saw his friends. The guards would be looking for him so he just left a message for James, who was in charge, and the other believers, and moved on.

57

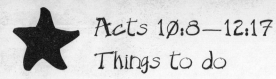

Travelling along

Get a long strip of paper and draw a road on it. Draw signposts along the road and write or draw pictures of the big events of your life so far. For example, show your birth date on the first post, your first day at school on the second, the first time you heard about Jesus on the third, and so on. Draw a final signpost pointing along the road to the things you are looking forward to doing in the future.

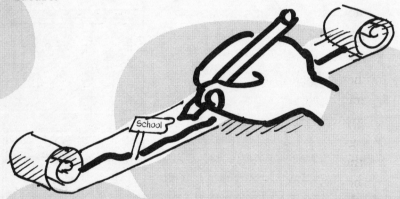

Toby + Trish — Travelling along

I'm going to the beach. Coming, Boomerang?

I'm going to the park. Coming, Boomerang?

Typical! It all comes at once!

Set apart
Acts 13:1-5

The Holy Spirit said to them, 'Set apart for me Barnabas and Saul, to do the work to which I have called them.' They fasted and prayed, placed their hands on them, and sent them off.
(Verses 2b–3)

At the beginning of term, your teacher may choose several children to do special jobs. One may give out the pencils, another may collect the books, another may be the class messenger and so on. Sometimes people are called out in assembly and given badges for doing the most important jobs.

> I haven't time to play. I'm reading in assembly tomorrow

God had special work for Saul and Barnabas to do. The Christian leaders chose them to go to Cyprus to teach about Jesus. They met together to pray and lay hands upon them before they went off. Saul and Barnabas knew that they would have a lot to do, so they took John Mark with them. He probably knew Jesus so he would have been a great help in their work.

My conjuring tricks never work!

Success in Cyprus
Acts 13:6-12

The governor called Barnabas and Saul before him because he wanted to hear the word of God. But they were opposed by the magician Elymas... who tried to turn the governor away from the faith.
(Verses 7b–8)

So, the first foreign journey was to the island of Cyprus. This may have been Barnabas' idea. He came from Cyprus so it was natural that he would want to tell his own relations and friends all about Jesus.

Cyprus was a Roman province. It was sometimes called the 'Happy Isle' because the climate was so perfect that people could find everything they needed to lead full and easy lives. But Saul never chose the easy way. He and Barnabas went straight to Paphos to meet the governor, Sergius Paulus. Most great men, even intelligent ones like Sergius Paulus, kept a magician to tell fortunes and deal with magic and spells. Elymas could see that if the governor became a Christian, he would lose his power and his job.

We cannot tell what will happen to us in the future. We know that God's care for us is much greater than any magic or superstition.

Thank you, dear Lord, that you look after us all the time. Amen

A change of name in Pisidia
Acts 13:13-32

After the reading from the Law of Moses, the officials of the synagogue sent them a message: 'Brothers and sisters, we want you to speak to the people if you have a message of encouragement for them.' Paul stood up, motioned with his hand, and began to speak. (Verses 15–16)

My uncle's name is John but his family call him Jack, so he is my Uncle Jack. Lots of people have two names, one that they have on their birth certificate and another one that their families use. People named Susan are often called 'Sue'. Michelle is sometimes altered to 'Shelly' or Michael becomes 'Mick'.

Up to this time in Acts, Paul has been called Saul. In those days, nearly all Jews had two names, a Jewish one which they were called by their family and friends, and a Greek one by which they were generally known. Paul used Saul, his Jewish name, at home but Paul in the wider world. He has now accepted that God wants him to teach people who were not Jewish about Jesus, so from this moment onwards he always uses his Greek name, 'Paul'.

It's Sunday, so I'm calling you Patricia

OK, Tobias!

Today Pisidia.
Tomorrow the world!

A light for the Gentiles
Acts 13:42-48

*Paul and Barnabas spoke out even more boldly:
'It was necessary that the word of God should
be spoken first to you. But since you reject it
and do not consider yourselves worthy of eternal
life, we will leave you and go to the Gentiles.'
(Verse 46)*

Kevin trained boys in a football club. They had blue shirts and met every Saturday. Soon, lots of other boys wanted to play as well. Then Alan, who was in charge, said that they could only be members if they had blue shirts. Kevin was angry. He said, 'I want everyone to play football. If you will only have members who can afford the shirts, I will start another club.' The boys were really pleased that they could join the new club. It soon became the best club in the town.

Paul had always preached at the Jewish synagogues. This time the leaders argued with him, so Paul left them and went instead to preach to the Gentiles who welcomed him. Paul decided that the good news of Jesus was for the whole world.

Popularity and protest
Acts 13:49—14:7

The word of the Lord spread everywhere in that region. But the Jews stirred up the leading men of the city and the Gentile women of high social standing who worshipped God. (Verses 49–50a)

There were three groups of people who were God-fearers. Philip met the Ethiopian who travelled all the way to the temple to worship God. Peter went to Cornelius, a Roman centurion who prayed and led a good life. Now Luke tells us about wealthy Gentile women who worshipped God. The Jewish leaders persuaded them to turn their husbands against Paul and Barnabas, so the two apostles had to move on. They are now in real danger because they have left the cities where the Romans kept order. They could be attacked at any time by excited crowds stirred up by the Jewish leaders.

Paul and Barnabas were very brave men. It always takes courage to be a Christian, because it takes courage to take a way that is different from everyone else's.

Brave people feel afraid, but go on in spite of it.

EXAM ROOM

Acts 13:1—14:7
Things to do

My job for God

God gave Paul and Barnabas special jobs to do. Make a wheel to show something that you do which is God's work. It may be something you do at your church, or being kind to someone, or helping at home or school.

Copy the wheel diagrams on to card by drawing two circles with a pair of compasses, or by drawing round a saucer. Mark the centre of both cards. On one card, cut away one section and write 'My job for God' on the remainder of the circle. On the other, mark the sections and write or draw something you do in each section. Fasten the two cards together with a split-pin paper fastener and turn the dial to show what you will do for God today.

My job for God

making my bed

dishes

reading to small sister

sharing

Toby + Trish   Paper round

I'm getting a paper round

You deliver 'em. I'll read 'em

Painted by Trish

Made by God

Mistaken identity
Acts 14:8-18

When the crowds saw what Paul had done, they started shouting in their own Lycaonian language, 'The gods have become like men and have come down to us!' They gave Barnabas the name Zeus, and Paul the name Hermes, because he was the chief speaker. (Verses 11–12)

There was a Lycaonian legend that two gods, called Zeus and Hermes, came to earth in disguise. They asked for shelter but nobody would help them until two peasants, Philimon and Baucis, welcomed them into their home. The gods were so angry with the Lycaonians that they killed all of them except Philimon and Baucis, whom they made guardians of a splendid temple. So when Paul healed the cripple, the people thought that he and Barnabas could be gods, and made sure they had a big welcome!

Paul and Barnabas were in difficulty. These people did not know about the one true God. Paul reminded them that God is the creator, who gives rain to make the crops grow for food and all good things.

Lord God, help us to look at our wonderful world and remember that you created it all. Amen

Real promises
Acts 14:21-28

Paul and Barnabas preached the Good News in Derbe and won many disciples. Then they went back to Lystra, to Iconium, and on to Antioch in Pisidia… When they arrived in Antioch, they gathered the people of the church together and told them about all that God had done with them and how he had opened the way for the Gentiles to believe. (Verses 21 and 27)

Yesterday, I got a letter. It said, 'Open immediately! You have won £1,000!' When I opened it, I found that I was only one of a number of people who might have won £1,000. If I bought a lot of books, I could enter a prize draw with several thousand other people. If my name were chosen, I would win the £1,000! It was an empty promise.

Paul was honest. He never made empty promises. He warned the Christians that there would be difficulties. But he appointed leaders to help them. And he encouraged them by telling them all that God had done for them since they last met. The same is true for us today. We need to help and encourage each other. And Paul reminds us that God always keeps his promises.

The meeting at Jerusalem
Acts 15:1–21

Some men came from Judea to Antioch and started teaching the believers, 'You cannot be saved unless you are circumcised as the Law of Moses requires.' Paul and Barnabas got into a fierce argument with them about this, so it was decided that Paul and Barnabas and some of the others in Antioch should go to Jerusalem and see the apostles and elders about this matter. (Verses 1–2)

When people don't agree, they can stop being friends or they can find an answer which satisfies everyone.

There were two types of Christians—those who went to the synagogue and obeyed the Jewish laws, and those who knew nothing about being Jewish. They were arguing about whether these non-Jewish Christians had to become Jews or could be Christians in their own right. A meeting was held in Jerusalem to sort it out.

It was decided that Christians did not have to be Jews, but had to keep some of their laws. This was an answer that satisfied everyone.

RULES OF THE HOUSE
Homework
Dishes
Clean room
Bedtime

Mum says if we're good we can talk about it

67

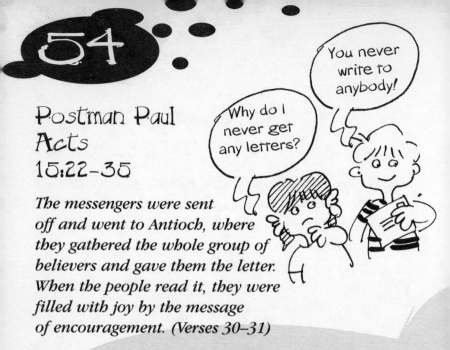

54

Postman Paul
Acts
15:22-35

The messengers were sent off and went to Antioch, where they gathered the whole group of believers and gave them the letter. When the people read it, they were filled with joy by the message of encouragement. (Verses 30–31)

How quickly can you send a message? You can pick up the telephone and speak at once. Some people can use e-mail, which takes a few minutes. A letter to any part of the world only takes a few days.

James had to tell the Gentile Christians that they did not have to become Jews. He wrote a long letter for Paul and Barnabas to take back to Antioch and, in case the people there wanted to argue again, he sent Judas and Silas to help to explain it.

It would have taken several weeks for Paul and Barnabas to travel from Jerusalem to Antioch. How excited the Christians there must have been to see them again with their new friends, Judas and Silas, and to receive such an encouraging reply.

Mark gets a second chance
Acts 15:36-41

Barnabas took Mark and sailed off for Cyprus,
while Paul chose Silas and left, commended by
the believers to the care of the Lord's grace.
(Verses 39b–40)

Some people go to the same place for their holidays each year. Others like to go to new places. My son, Andrew, bought a tent and a bicycle and went off to southern Africa to see what it was like. He made lots of friends and had wonderful adventures.

Paul was an adventurer who could never stay long in one place. Having sorted out the church in Antioch, it was time to take to the road again. This time, though, it was without his friend Barnabas. Barnabas wanted to take Mark along with them, but Paul felt that Mark was unreliable. So Barnabas and Mark went off to Cyprus and Paul took Silas as a companion.

Barnabas was a warm and friendly person. He believed in Mark and gave him a second chance. Mark eventually showed he was right.

> I'll only take you if this time you promise not to run off with the ball

Acts 14:8—15:41
Things to do

Catch the post

Think who would like a letter to cheer them up. Perhaps an older person, or someone in hospital or living alone. Cut out happy pictures from a magazine, or do a painting to send with your letter to show that you care. Ask an adult to help you address the letter and post it.

Toby + Trish — Nice surprise

Why are you posting half a bar of chocolate to yourself?

So I've got some left for tomorrow

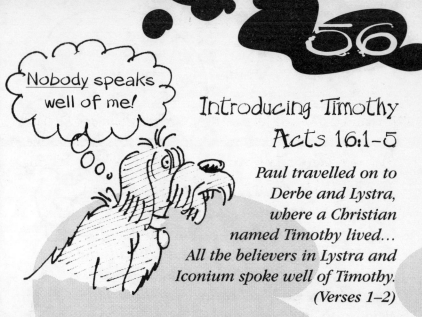

Nobody speaks well of me!

Introducing Timothy
Acts 16:1-5

Paul travelled on to Derbe and Lystra, where a Christian named Timothy lived... All the believers in Lystra and Iconium spoke well of Timothy. (Verses 1–2)

I expect that you sometimes help your parents with jobs. That is how you will learn to do useful things like cooking food or decorating a room. Paul would have been looking for someone to take Mark's place. He must have been so happy to find that Timothy had grown into a fine young man who could help Paul on his travels and learn to become a leader himself in time.

Timothy became a very special friend to Paul. He went with him on many journeys and eventually became the leader of the Christians in Ephesus. Paul taught him everything that he knew and wrote two letters to him which are full of help and advice on how to be a good leader. You can find them with Paul's other letters after the book of Acts in your Bible.

57

**Enter Doctor
Luke!**

Acts 16:6-10

*That night Paul had a vision in which
he saw a Macedonian standing and
begging him, 'Come over to Macedonia
and help us!' As soon as Paul had this vision, we
got ready to leave for Macedonia, because we
decided that God had called us to preach the Good
News to the people there. (Verses 9–10)*

Suddenly, all the doors are shut. The Holy Spirit stopped
Paul preaching in Asia. But then came the vision asking
him to travel into Europe to the people of Macedonia.
How did the Holy Spirit send these messages to Paul?

Read the verses at the top of this page again slowly.
Who are the 'we' that are mentioned twice? You may
remember that Luke, the writer of the book of Acts, went
on some of Paul's journeys. Suddenly, Luke is here. Luke
was a doctor. Perhaps he met Paul at this time because
Paul was ill and could not travel into Asia as he hoped.
And who was the Macedonian that Paul saw in his vision?
Perhaps it was Luke!

It is a wonderful thought that Paul could use even
illness to listen to God.

Europe's first Christians
Acts 16:11-15

On the Sabbath we went out of the city to the river-side, where we thought there would be a place where Jews gathered for prayer. We sat down and talked to the women who gathered there. (Verse 13)

Philippi was a Roman colony. It was hundreds of miles from Rome but it was built to show local people what a privilege it was to belong to the powerful Roman Empire.

Wherever Paul travelled, he always looked first for a Jewish synagogue. There was not one in Philippi, so the Jewish women met for an open-air service by the river. Paul, Silas and Luke went there to talk to them. Lydia was a wealthy businesswoman, buying and selling an expensive purple dye. She learned about Jesus at that open-air service. Immediately she did two things. First, she shared her faith with her family and servants—they were baptized with her. Second, she invited Paul and his companions to stay with her. The Christian faith is a shared faith. A Christian home is a welcoming home.

The slave girl
Acts 16:16-24

One day as we were going to the place of prayer, we were met by a young servant woman who had an evil spirit that enabled her to predict the future. She earned a lot of money for her owners by telling fortunes… Paul turned around and said to the spirit, 'In the name of Jesus Christ I order you to come out of her!' The spirit went out of her that very moment. (Verses 16 and 18b)

If someone you love has been very ill, you will know how happy you were when they got well again. You would expect the people who looked after this young woman to be delighted when Paul made her well. Not a bit of it! They were so angry that they had Paul and Silas thrown into jail.

We think differently about this kind of illness from the way people did in Paul's day, but, like Paul, we would want the poor girl to be made well. The really sad thing is that Paul and Silas were punished for doing something good.

Yesterday, we read how Paul baptized a wealthy woman's family. Today he heals a poor sick girl in the name of Jesus. Luke shows us that everyone, however rich or poor, can come to know and follow Jesus.

Into prison
Acts 16:25-33

*About midnight Paul and Silas were praying and
singing hymns to God, and the other prisoners were
listening to them. Suddenly there was a violent
earthquake, which shook the prison to its
foundations. At once all the doors opened,
and the chains fell off all the prisoners.
(Verses 25–26)*

Philippi was in that part of the world that we now call
Turkey, and it still has earth tremors such as the one that
happened when Paul and Silas were in prison that night.
They would probably have been beaten and had their feet,
hands and necks put into holes in stocks. Very unpleasant!
But they still said their prayers and sang hymns.

After the quake freed them, the jailer knew that if his
prisoners escaped he would be imprisoned and maybe die.
Paul and Silas did not want this to happen so they stayed
there.

That night, the jailer and his whole family became
Christians. He arranged for
Paul's and Silas' wounds
to be bathed and for
them to have a meal.
The jailer's despair was
turned into joy.

Sometimes the floor shakes when we sing hymns 'cos we stamp our feet!

Acts 16:1-33
Things to do

Down in the dungeon

Sit in a circle with your friends. Call one person 'Paul', the next 'Silas', the next 'Luke' and the next 'Timothy'. Number the remaining people in the circle. Start clapping slowly while 'Paul' starts by saying, for example, 'Paul to Luke'. 'Luke' then says 'Luke to 4', and so on. If anyone stops or gives the wrong name, everyone shouts 'Dungeon!' That person then sits in the middle until someone else makes a mistake and takes his or her place. The game stops when you are tired. Have fun!

clap clap clap clap

Toby + Trish — In the dark

Toby, there's something heavy landed on top of my bed. Has the roof fallen in?

No, it's only Boomerang

Standing up for what is right
Acts 16:35-40

Paul said to the police officers, 'We were not found guilty of any crime, yet they whipped us in public— and we are Roman citizens! Then they threw us in prison. And now they want to send us away secretly. Not likely! The Roman officials themselves must come here and let us out.' (Verse 37)

Paul and Silas had been born with a very special honour. They were Roman citizens. This meant that they had special rights and privileges. Whereas others could be punished by being beaten, Roman citizens couldn't. So what had happened to Paul and Silas was against the law, and Paul makes a point of telling the authorities so. The Roman officials had to apologize. Then they wanted Paul to leave as quickly as possible. But Paul was not in a hurry! He and Silas went to Lydia's house to visit their new friends who were the first members of a strong and generous church.

People are sometimes treated badly because they are Christians. That does not mean that they should put up with it. Paul and Silas were not prepared to be treated in a way which was against the law. Christians must always stand up for what is right.

On to Thessalonica
Acts 17:1–9

Paul and Silas travelled on through Amphipolis and Apollonia and came to Thessalonica, where there was a synagogue. According to his usual habit Paul went to the synagogue. (Verses 1–2a)

I live near to the junction of three motorways, so I can visit friends in all parts of the country very easily. I can also get to two airports and the Channel Tunnel in an hour, so, if I had time, I could get up in the morning and be almost anywhere in the world by the afternoon!

Paul's journey to Thessalonica sounds like an easy trip, but it was over a hundred miles and took several days. But the coming of the Christian faith to Thessalonica was an important event. The great Roman road from the Adriatic Sea to the Middle East was called the Egnetian Way. It was this road that ran through Thessalonica. Once Christianity was established there, it could easily travel east and west. The Egnetian Way became the highway of the kingdom of God.

Why do you always pull the wrong way?

All stirred up
Acts 17:10–15

As soon as night came, the believers sent Paul and Silas to Berea. When they arrived, they went to the synagogue. The people there were more open-minded than the people in Thessalonica. They listened to the message with great eagerness, and every day they studied the Scriptures to see if what Paul said was really true. (Verses 10–11)

Notice that Paul always starts by going to the synagogue, and he uses the scriptures for his teaching. He expects his hearers to study them to see if what he says is true. Then, when the time comes for him to move on, he has to leave his friends Silas and Timothy behind. They probably continued the teaching.

Paul was in continual danger. He was imprisoned in Philippi, smuggled out of Thessalonica, and now has to escape from Berea, leaving two of his closest companions behind. Because Jesus had been crucified, the Jewish leaders could not accept that he was God's Son. In their eyes, this shameful death meant he was a really bad person. So, although Luke's story may read as if the Jewish leaders were gangs of thugs, the sad thing is that they really believed that they were doing what God wanted in trying to stop Paul.

64

The unknown god

Why does a brown cow give white milk, when it only eats green grass?

Acts: 17:16-31

'As I walked through your city and looked at the places where you worship, I found an altar on which is written, "To an Unknown God". That which you worship, then, even though you do not know it, is what I now proclaim to you.' (Verse 23)

Every day, some new discovery is made—the cure for an illness, a new understanding about the way the world is formed or why our weather is changing. The work for this is done in our universities by people discussing, researching and seeking new answers.

Paul finds himself alone in Athens which, in his day, was the greatest university in the world. Everyone was talking about new ideas, so they listened eagerly to Paul's teaching. He is called to the Aeropagus, the highest court, to explain his faith. Paul can fit his story to any situation so he starts with the Greeks' search for 'the unknown God'. He explains that God is not unknown or distant. He has guided history and we are his children. He raised Jesus from the dead and will be our judge.

Don't give up!
Acts 18:1-11

*After this, Paul left Athens and went on to Corinth.
There he met a Jew named Aquila, born in Pontus,
who had recently come from Italy with his wife
Priscilla... Paul went to see them, and stayed and
worked with them, because he earned his living by
making tents, just as they did. (Verses 1–3)*

Luke gives us a vivid picture of the sort of person that
Paul was. He was a Jewish rabbi and, unlike our priests
or ministers, rabbis could not be paid but had to have a
trade. Paul was a tent-maker, so he would have worked
with leather and cloth, and been a skilled craftsman.
Sometimes the believers invited Paul to stay with them so
that he could spend all of his time telling
people about Jesus. But Paul still always
earned his own living.

Don't
give up,
Toby!

The people who lived in Corinth were
mostly unfriendly and gave
Paul a hard time. But, just
when he felt like giving up,
God spoke to him. 'Don't
give up; I am with you,' was
the message, and this gave Paul
courage to stay there for one and a
half years, teaching about Jesus.

Acts 16:35—18:11
Things to do

The unknown God

Paul found an altar 'To the Unknown God' in Athens. Take a piece of paper. Write at the top, 'Things I know about God'. Then think of six things that you know about him. Write them down and go and tell someone.

Things I know about God

1
2
3
4
5
6

Toby + Trish — Unknown cereal

This is breakfast cereal 'x'. You've got to guess what it is.

It's cornflakes. I *always* have cornflakes

Paul thanks God
Acts 18:18-23

Paul stayed on with the believers in Corinth for many days, then left them and sailed off with Priscilla and Aquila for Syria. Before sailing from Cenchreae he had his head shaved because of a vow he had taken. (Verse 18)

Can you remember a time you were given a special birthday present? Great! Then your mum said, 'Now you must write to say "Thank you".' That is not so much fun—in fact, you may even forget to thank the person who gave it to you.

Paul is now on his way home, but he stopped at Cenchreae to have his head shaved. When a Jew wanted to thank God for a special blessing, he took the Nazarite vow. For thirty days he did not eat meat or drink wine and he let his hair grow. Then, he made an offering to God and his hair was shaved off. Paul had been through so much on his journeys, but he remembered to thank God for keeping him safe and allowing him to teach so many people about Jesus.

What do you say for borrowing my skateboard?

THANKs

When it's tea-time, Boomerang knows the quickest way home!

Introducing Apollos
Acts 18:24-28

At that time a Jew named Apollos,
who had been born in Alexandria,
came to Ephesus. He was an eloquent speaker and
had a thorough knowledge of the Scriptures. He
had been instructed in the Way of the Lord, and
with great enthusiasm he proclaimed and taught
correctly the facts about Jesus. (Verses 24–25)

I expect that some of you walk home from school. Before you started doing this, your mum probably told you the correct route and the best place to cross the road. You may also have been told places to avoid because they were dangerous.

One of the commonest ways of describing Christianity at the time of Paul was to call it 'The Way'. It shows that being a Christian is not just about believing certain things—it is about doing them. Being a Christian is rather like going on a journey, following the route that Jesus has taken. Sometimes we follow it well. At other times we take a wrong turning.

Apollos had the knowledge to show the Jews that Jesus was God's Son. But he needed to learn that Jesus opens the way to God.

What kind of baptism?
Acts 19:1-7

*'What kind of baptism did you receive?' Paul asked.
'The baptism of John,' they answered. Paul said,
'The baptism of John was for those who turned
from their sins; and he told the people of Israel to
believe in the one who was coming after him—that
is, in Jesus.' When they heard this, they were
baptized in the name of the Lord Jesus.*
(Verses 3–5)

There are two reasons why Mum sends you to the
bathroom to wash. One is because we all need to wash to
stay clean and healthy. The other one is because she wants
you to look extra smart for a special occasion like a party.

The reason why John baptized people was a bit like the
first washing. They needed to turn
away from doing wrong—to
have their sins washed away,
like washing dirt off our
hands. Baptism in the name
of Jesus is different. Yes, we
still need to turn away from doing
wrong but we can also celebrate
that Jesus has given us a fresh start
and his Holy Spirit will live in us
and change our lives.

85

Burning the books
Acts:19:13-20

Many of the believers came, publicly admitting and revealing what they had done. Many of those who had practised magic brought their books together and burnt them in public. (Verses 18–19a)

We all know some superstitions. For example, the number seven and black cats are supposed to bring luck. We know that God is bigger than any number or the most beautiful of black cats, but there are still some people who pay money to have fortunes told or cross their fingers for good luck.

Some of the people who practised magic in Ephesus were probably convinced that they had special powers. But, when they saw the effect of trying to use the name of Jesus, they realized that they had got it all wrong. They were very brave because they admitted their mistakes and then burned all their books and charms which they needed to earn their living.

You may know people who have given up a bad habit— like smoking. It needs courage and it is always best to make a clean break.

I'm giving up Brussels sprouts

That's no good. You don't like them anyway!

Riot in Ephesus!
Acts 19:21-41

It was at this time that there was serious trouble in Ephesus because of the Way of the Lord. A certain silversmith named Demetrius made silver models of the temple of the goddess Artemis, and his business brought a great deal of profit to the workers. (Verses 23–24)

When you go on holiday, you probably bring home a souvenir like a T-shirt. Ephesus was the greatest city in Asia, with public buildings, a huge theatre and the temple of the goddess Diana Artemis. Pilgrims came there from all over the world and they wanted to take home souvenirs, silver images of the goddess and her shrine.

This is a thrilling story. When you have read it, think about the characters. First there is Demetrius. He claims to protect the honour of Artemis but is more worried about his business. Then there is the town clerk who stops the riot. If Rome discovered that there had been civil disorder, he would be in serious trouble. Then there is Paul. He is quite the opposite. He wants to face the mob. For him, personal safety came last.

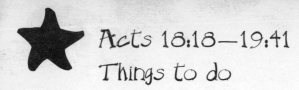

Acts 18:18—19:41
Things to do

Make a spinner

Using a saucer as a template, cut out a circle of card. Colour one side with fire colours—red, orange and yellow. On the other side, write in a different colour, 'Hear the word of the Lord'. Find the middle of the circle and make two small holes either side of it, about 3 cm apart. Thread through a piece of string and tie the ends. Holding the string firmly, set the card spinning by swinging it forward in a circular motion to 'wind it up' and then pulling on the string.

I think we'll go out through the back door of the changing-room at half-time

A tactical withdrawal
Acts 20:1-6

After the uproar died down, Paul called together the believers and with words of encouragement said goodbye to them. Then he left and went on to Macedonia.
(Verse 1)

'Never fight a battle you can't win' is good advice. Paul had wanted to speak to thousands of angry workers in Ephesus, but now he realizes that it is too dangerous to stay, so he slips away and continues his travels.

Paul travels for several months. He continues to teach and encourage new believers but he is also collecting money to support the needy Christians in Jerusalem. Each one of Paul's companions was carrying gifts of money from his church. So, there is double danger. Paul foils a plot to murder him by changing his route but there is still the danger of their being attacked and robbed.

But, at Philippi, there is Luke to greet them! It was the time of the festival of Unleavened Bread, the Passover, so the date would have been the middle of April.

72

Dropping off
Acts 20:7-12

A young man named Eutychus was sitting in the window, and as Paul kept on talking, Eutychus got sleepier and sleepier, until he finally went sound asleep and fell from the third storey to the ground. When they picked him up, he was dead. (Verse 9)

A friend of mine is absent-minded. One day he walked along a sea wall and forgot to stop. He walked off the end into the water! We all had a good laugh—once we knew that he was not badly hurt.

Eutychus had gone to a Christian friend's house for the fellowship meal. He was excited because the great teacher Paul would be there. He curled up on the floor by the window. Windows were not glazed but had wooden shutters. The room was lit by oil lamps. It got stuffier and stuffier until Eutychus fell asleep. Unfortunately, he was leaning against the wooden shutter so he literally dropped off to the ground below. There was a gasp, laughter, and then screams as people thought he was dead.

Paul leapt downstairs and pressed his ear against Eutychus' heart. There was still a pulse. Then he stayed there until the next morning to check that he was recovered and that someone would take him home.

No. It was TV last night that wasn't boring enough!

Shorter by sea
Acts 20:13-16

Paul had decided to sail on past Ephesus, so as not to lose any time in the province of Asia. He was in a hurry to arrive in Jerusalem by the day of Pentecost, if at all possible.
(Verse 16)

When I was small, we had our Queen's coronation. The girls next door were going to wait in the crowds all night to see the procession. I wanted to go too, but I was too young. When I grew up I decided that I would not miss the Queen's silver jubilee, so I waited for hours to see her go past in the golden state coach. And it was worth the wait!

Paul must have felt like that when the plot to kill him prevented his getting to Jerusalem for the Feast of the Passover. He was still a Jew and this great feast was very important for him. So, he did the next best thing—he made sure that he could be at the Feast of Weeks, Pentecost, to celebrate that instead.

You would be a great guard dog if you could stay awake!

Keep watch!
Acts 20:17-31

Paul sent a message to Ephesus, asking the elders of the church to meet him. When they arrived, he said to them, '...keep watch over yourselves and over all the flock which the Holy Spirit has placed in your care. Be shepherds of the church of God, which he made his own through the blood of his son.' (Verses 17 and 28)

If you have a new bicycle, you take great care of it. You lock it up so that it cannot be stolen and you try not to let it get too dirty and scratched. Why? Because someone in your family had to pay a lot of money for it, and maybe even had to go without other things.

Paul gives his last speech to his new Christian friends in Ephesus and he says, 'Keep watch.' He orders them to take great care of all the believers who belong to God's Church. This is not just because people should look after each other, but for a very special reason. Jesus bought their freedom, and ours, by giving his life for us on the cross.

Dear God, help us to remember that Jesus' love is worth far more than all the treasures in the world. Amen

A sad farewell
Acts 20:32-38

When Paul finished, he knelt down with them and prayed. They were all crying as they hugged him and kissed him goodbye. (Verses 36–37)

Miss Howard was a new teacher and her class did not like her. But, as she taught them, they began to enjoy her lessons. Some of them were very interesting and she was really a nice person—provided you got on with your work!

At the end of term, Miss Howard told her class that she was going home to Australia. Some children cried, and they were all sad that she was leaving them. 'You have been our best teacher,' they said.

Perhaps that is a little like Paul's visits to Ephesus. At first, he met with a riot. Then gradually his teaching got across and, when he finally left, there was a strong church—an active group of Christians, who were sad to see him go and even went to the ship to see him off.

> Kylie's going to another school next term... sob... sob...

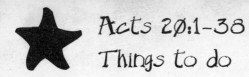

Acts 20:1-38
Things to do

Smoking lamps

Eutychus fell asleep and toppled out of the window because the room was hot and smoky with the heat from the lamps. Copy one of the lamps in the picture and colour it with yellow flame and black smoke. Imagine the smoky lamps being the only light in a room full of people. How sleepy you would be!

Toby + Trish

I must have dropped off!

Trish, dear sister, I'm giving you my new Walkman and CD player

I've woken up to reality!

...and she's getting a super new uniform! ... wail ...

Greek islands

Acts 21:1–6

We found some believers and stayed with them for about a week. By the power of the Spirit they told Paul not to go to Jerusalem. But when our time with them was over, we left and went on our way. All of them, together with their wives and children, went with us out of the city to the beach, where we all knelt and prayed. (Verses 4–5)

We have now got to one of the turning-points in the adventure of Paul. The story gathers pace. Paul sails from island to island, stopping for only a few days at a time. Everywhere he goes, there are groups of Christians to greet him. The good news about Jesus has spread ahead of Paul and he must have been so happy to find churches springing up everywhere he went.

But there are two shadows over this exciting and happy scene. The believers in Tyre warn Paul not to go to Jerusalem. Something bad will happen to him there. Then Luke tells us all about their new friends praying with them on the beach before saying goodbye. We realize that Paul will never see them again.

Agabus acts it out
Acts 21:7–16

We had been in Caesarea for several days when a prophet named Agabus arrived from Judea. He came to us, took Paul's belt, tied up his own feet and hands with it, and said, '… The owner of this belt will be tied up in this way by the Jews in Jerusalem, and they will hand him over to the Gentiles.' (Verses 10–11)

You may sometimes do drama at school when you act without talking. This is called 'mime'. You describe an event or mood without using words. The actions are usually more powerful than just talking.

Agabus is a prophet, a person who warns people and nations of what will happen if they behave in a particular way. They were often seen as speaking for God. If Jewish prophets wanted to tell of something that they believed would happen and could not find the right words, they would dramatize the message instead. This would make people notice it. So, in front of everyone, Agabus takes Paul's belt and ties up his own hands and feet with it. The message is clear. If Paul goes to Jerusalem, he too will be tied up and handed over to his enemies.

A meeting with James
Acts 21:17-26

When we arrived in Jerusalem, the believers welcomed us warmly. The next day Paul went with us to see James; and all the church elders were present. (Verses 17–18)

Harry and Alex were going out with Granny. Harry wanted to go to the zoo but Alex wanted to go swimming. 'I know,' said Granny. 'There is a swimming pool in a park where there are also some animals. We will spend a little time at each.' So they were both content. This is called a compromise.

Paul had given James and the elders the money he had collected for the poor. James warned Paul that some people said he was teaching the Jews to ignore the Jewish laws. He suggested that he should use some of the money for a thanksgiving rite to show people that he was really genuine. Paul did not want to do it but he realized that it would stop the accusations. So he compromised. Just like Harry and Alex.

We'll share the skateboard. You have it when it rains and I'll have it when it doesn't

In the hands of the mob
Acts 21:27-36

Some Jews from the province of Asia saw Paul in the Temple. They stirred up the whole crowd...Confusion spread through the whole city, and the people all ran together, seized Paul, and dragged him out of the Temple. At once the Temple doors were closed. (Verses 27 and 30)

Poor Paul! Having finally got to Jerusalem and been welcomed by James and the other Christians, he finds that the money intended for the poor has to be used to 'prove' that he is a loyal Jew. So, off he goes with four companions to the temple to carry out the ceremony. It is just ending when he is spotted and the accusations start again.

Of all Paul's dangers, this is probably the greatest. He is dragged out of the temple by a mob and the one cry he can hear is, 'Kill him!' Again, the power and order of the Roman Empire come to the rescue. Soldiers carry him out of the crowds by holding him above their heads like a shield. Paul is alive but now he has to answer to the Roman commander.

Paul tells his story
Acts 21:37-4Ø

'I am a Jew, born in Tarsus in Cilicia, a citizen of an important city. Please let me speak to the people.' (Verse 39)

'Out of the frying pan, into the fire!' Roman justice saves Paul from being stoned by a furious mob. But the soldiers think that he is an Egyptian terrorist, who has led a gang called the Dagger-bearers, so they arrest him. When Paul speaks to them in Greek, which was the language of educated people, and says who he is and where he comes from, the Roman captain allows him to speak to the crowd.

Most people would have been so relieved to be rescued that they would have thanked their rescuers and got right away from the danger. Not so with Paul. He turns to the mob, makes a gesture for silence and, amazingly, he gets it. Paul, using their native language of Hebrew, tells his Christian story.

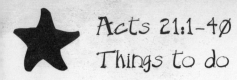

Acts 21:1-40
Things to do

Acting it out

Agabus mimed a warning to Paul to let him know there was danger ahead. Mime something to your friends and ask them to work out what it is. It does not have to be a warning, but something like eating a meal, playing football, or feeling tired. The first person to give the correct answer takes a turn to mime a fresh action, and so on.

Toby + Trish | Acting it out

I've got a part in the school panto. I'm the front end of the horse

I don't want an autograph—just give me a hoof-print

This is how it happened
Acts 21:1-21

'I am a Jew, born in Tarsus in Cilicia, but brought up here in Jerusalem as a student of Gamaliel. I received strict instruction in the Law of our ancestors and was just as dedicated to God as are all of you who are here today... "Go," the Lord said to me, "for I will send you far away to the Gentiles."' (Verses 3 and 21)

Paul tells his life story to the mob, and they stop to listen to him. First, he shows them that he is trustworthy. He is a Jew from Tarsus, a city with a famous university. He studied with the great teacher Gamaliel. Then he arrested people who opposed the Law, and even assisted in the death of Stephen.

But then Paul met Jesus on the road to Damascus and it changed his life. We have read about it already, but here Paul tells it to the crowd as it happened to him, and says one thing we have not read before. Paul says that he wanted to stay with the Jews, God's chosen people. They did not listen to him, so God sent him to the Gentiles. God's love as shown in Jesus is for everyone.

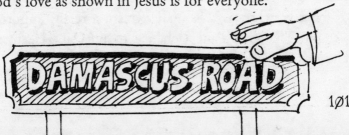

I am a Roman citizen
Acts 22:22-29

*At once the men who were going to question Paul
drew back from him; and the commander was
frightened when he realized that Paul was a Roman
citizen and that he had put him in chains.
(Verse 29)*

Emma was driving home
when she found that there
had been a traffic accident.
All the cars had to stop
and wait. Suddenly, Emma
moved out of the queue and
down the wrong side of the
road. 'Stop!' called a policeman. 'I am a doctor,' replied
Emma. 'Let me through and I may be able to help!'

Emma could have waited with everyone else but she
gave the policeman a good reason why she should be
treated differently. She was a doctor. She could help the
injured people while they waited for an ambulance.

Paul could have said nothing and been whipped. But
there was good reason why he should be treated
differently. He was a Roman citizen, a really important
person. This gave Paul a chance to put his case to the
Council and be a witness for Jesus.

Don't worry, Boomerang, I'll guide you down this busy street

Don't be afraid!
Acts 22:30— 23:11

That night the Lord stood by Paul and said, 'Don't be afraid! You have given your witness for me here in Jerusalem, and you must also do the same in Rome.' (Verse 11)

Saints are usually seen in stained-glass windows—sombre figures in long robes, with haloes around their heads. But when you read about them in the Bible, you find a very different picture. They are tough and determined people who are prepared to do almost anything to follow Jesus.

Paul takes an enormous risk in the way he answers the Council. Jews were considered to be unclean if they touched a dead body, so tombs were painted white to warn them to keep away. Paul suggests that Ananias is like a tomb, a white wall outside, but rotten inside. Then he sets the Pharisees and Sadducees against each other. Paul is fighting for his freedom with every trick he knows. But, afterwards, he has the inner assurance that God is beside him and that his witness will continue.

Paul had God on his side plus half an army!

Another plot foiled
Acts 23:12-24

Then the commander called two of his officers and said, 'Get two hundred soldiers ready to go to Caesarea, together with seventy horsemen and two hundred spearmen, and be ready to leave by nine o'clock tonight. Provide some horses for Paul to ride and get him safely through to the governor Felix.' (Verses 23–24)

This is a strange story! Jewish leaders, whose Law tells them not to kill, vow to murder Paul while the Romans protect him with half an army. Luke had a particular reason for writing it like this.

The Jewish leaders saw Paul as a threat to their beliefs. On the other hand, the Romans do not see him as a law-breaker, so they go to great lengths to protect him and to see that he has a fair trial from Felix the governor. Luke wrote his book for people who were ruled by the Romans. They would be reassured to read that those in power saw Paul and his fellow Christians as law-abiding people, not terrorists who were trying to undermine the structure of the Roman Empire.

Safe passage to Felix
Acts 23:25-35

They took Paul to Caesarea, delivered the letter to the governor, and handed Paul over to him. The governor read the letter and asked Paul what province he was from. When he found out that he was from Cilicia, he said, 'I will hear you when your accusers arrive.' (Verses 33–35a)

The Roman government was based in Caesarea, which was about sixty miles from Jerusalem. The journey as far as Antipatris was dangerous and the party could have been attacked, so a large number of soldiers went as far as there and then turned back. After that, the country was flat and open, so Paul would be safe with a small escort.

The letter from Claudius Lysias to Felix shows how the Romans were fair and were not going to get involved in local religious disputes. It reminds his readers that Paul has not broken any law. So, he should be safe, but he meets a different danger. Felix, the governor, was completely unscrupulous. His rule had been marked by cruelty and greed. It is to this rogue that Paul has to plead his case.

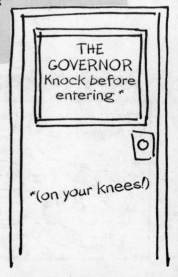

THE GOVERNOR
Knock before entering *

*(on your knees!)

Acts 21:1—23:35
Things to do

I am a Roman citizen

Paul was born a Roman citizen. We, too, are citizens of the country where we were born. On the inside cover of a passport are the words, 'To afford the bearer such assistance and protection as may be necessary.' This means that the government of our country asks that we should have help if we need it, wherever we are in the world. This would have been the same for Paul as a citizen of Rome.

Ask an adult to show you a passport and find out why it is important to have a passport when we travel abroad.

Toby + Trish — Passport to happiness

We're flying to Spain next year

Can't wait to swim in the Med

Can't wait to go into kennels!

Kylie's been going round saying bad things about me...

Tertullus states the case
Acts 24:1-9

Tertullus began to make his accusation, as follows: '...We found this man to be a dangerous nuisance; he starts riots among Jews all over the world and is a leader of the party of the Nazarenes.' (Verses 2 and 5)

Tertullus was a lawyer, a highly educated man who understood Roman and Jewish law. He has come with the Jewish leaders to bring their charges against Paul. Somehow, he has got to get Felix convinced that Paul is guilty.

So, Tertullus starts by flattering Felix and saying how grateful the Jews are for his leadership and reforms. This is untrue and Felix knows it. Then he twists the accusations against Paul, saying that he caused riots and led a group of trouble-makers, the Nazarenes. Tertullus knows that Rome would not tolerate riots. The empire was vast and a rebellion could spread like fire if it were not squashed immediately. There had been violence, but Paul had not caused it. Half-truths and twisted facts are far worse and harder to defend than outright lies.

87

Paul's defence
Acts 24:10-23

... but underneath she's worried about going to a new school

Then Felix, who was well informed about the Way, brought the hearing to a close. 'When Lysias the commander arrives,' he told them, 'I will decide your case.' He ordered the officer in charge of Paul to keep him under guard, but to give him some freedom and allow his friends to provide for his needs. (Verses 22–23)

Go around your house and knock on the doors, cupboards and other items. All of them will make different sounds. The strongest sound will be if you knock on something hollow that is not damaged, a wooden box or an empty glass. The sound rings out. If the object is cracked, it gives a dull sound.

Judges sometimes decide to believe a person because what they say has the 'ring of truth'. What they say sounds clear, like the sound of the glass or box. Paul's defence is like that. He had only been in Jerusalem for a few days, to pray in the temple and bring money for needy Christians. This could be true or untrue, but Felix recognizes the ring of truth in his words. He keeps him under guard but treats him well.

Felix takes his chance
Acts 24:24-27

*After some days Felix came with his wife Drusilla,
who was Jewish. He sent for Paul and listened to
him as he talked about faith in Christ Jesus.*
(Verse 24)

Félix was not unkind to Paul, but kept him under house
arrest. He sent for him regularly to listen to him in the
company of his Jewish wife, Drusilla. She was the
daughter of Herod and had been married before. Felix
must have been fascinated by Paul's teaching. Luke has
already told us that he was well informed about the Way,
a common name for the Christian faith. But Paul's words
had a ring of truth again. Hearing about goodness, self-
control and the day of judgment made this corrupt leader
uneasy.

Two years later, Felix's government was in such
disarray that he was recalled to Rome. He should have
released Paul from prison
but he left him there.
Luke's record of that one
injustice has made Felix
known as a scoundrel to
all Christians since then.

89

Paul appeals to Caesar
Acts 25:1-12

Three days after Festus arrived in the province, he went from Caesarea to Jerusalem, where the chief priests and the Jewish leaders brought their charges against Paul. They begged Festus to do them the favour of bringing Paul to Jerusalem, for they had made a plot to kill him on the way. (Verses 1–3)

Unlike Felix, Festus was an honest man. The Jewish leaders tried to persuade him to send Paul to Jerusalem so that they could ambush and kill him on the way. But Festus had a Roman sense of justice—he told them to come to Caesarea to present their case.

During Paul's trial, however, Festus wanted to keep in favour with the Jewish leaders, so he sounded Paul out about going to Jerusalem. Paul knew that he would not get justice there, so he used his greatest privilege as a Roman citizen. He appealed to the Emperor. This meant that he had to be taken to Rome, where Caesar would personally decide his fate.

So Paul, in very different circumstances from those of which he had dreamed, made the first step on the journey that would lead him to Rome.

Your Majesties, Honourable Governor. Here is... er... Paul. A tent-maker.

Courts and kings
Acts 25:13-27

The next day Agrippa and Bernice came with great pomp and ceremony and entered the audience hall with the military chiefs and the leading men of the city. Festus gave the order, and Paul was brought in. (Verse 23)

Sometimes we see pictures of grand ceremonies on television, full of colour and ceremony with bands playing and soldiers marching. How would you feel if you had to stand in front of the Royal Family? Scary!

King Agrippa and Queen Bernice had come to visit Festus, and Paul was called into the large assembly hall. Agrippa and Bernice would have been dressed in purple robes with gold coronets because they were royalty, and Festus would have worn his scarlet toga. Surrounding them were courtiers and the ceremonial guard. And there was Paul, a little tent-maker from Tarsus, worn and shabby with his hands in chains. He must have been terrified.

But Paul takes centre stage. These are the kings of the earth. He speaks for a heavenly king—Jesus, the greatest king of all.

Acts 24:1—25:27
Things to do

Put him in chains

Paul was always being chained up for his belief in Jesus. Make some chains like Christmas paper chains to show why Paul was happy to be in prison because of all that Jesus had done for us. You need paper, a pen and a glue stick. Cut the paper into strips. Write on each one something about Jesus.

Make the chains and hang them up in your bedroom to remind you of people who have gone to prison because they believe in Jesus.

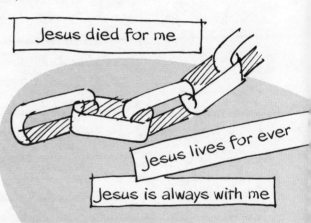

Jesus died for me

Jesus lives for ever

Jesus is always with me

Toby + Trish — Chain reaction

I thought chains weren't meant to come off

They're not

Well, my bicycle chain is always coming off.

Paul stands before Agrippa
Acts 26:1-18

Agrippa said to Paul, 'You have permission to speak on your own behalf.' Paul stretched out his hand and defended himself as follows: 'King Agrippa! I consider myself fortunate that today I am to defend myself before you from all the things the Jews accuse me of, particularly since you know so well all the Jewish customs and disputes. I ask you, then, to listen to me with patience.' (Verses 1–3)

If you go on a rollercoaster at a fun-fair, it starts slowly, then gets more and more frightening, but you can't get off.

Paul defended himself to the Jewish Council, then Felix, and now he stands in front of King Agrippa. Jesus had warned his friends, 'For my sake you will be brought to trial before rulers and kings, to tell the Good News to them and the Gentiles.' It is really happening and, like the rollercoaster, Paul can't get off.

Paul tells Agrippa how he sent Jesus' followers to prison and to their death. He does not claim to be a good person but shows how meeting the risen Jesus on the road to Damascus changed his life.

Dear Jesus, thank you that knowing you can make a bad person into a good one, and that this is still true today. Amen

Become what I am
Acts 26:19-32

Agrippa said to Paul, 'In this short time do you think you will make me a Christian?' 'Whether a short time or a long time,' Paul answered, 'my prayer to God is that you and all the rest of you who are listening to me today might become what I am—except, of course, for these chains!'
(Verses 28–29)

If a person defends himself in court, he concentrates on showing that he is innocent. Paul is different. He has already told King Agrippa of his evil past. Now he finishes by telling the king about Jesus and how he died and rose again for us.

And they cannot handle it. Festus claims that Paul is mad. Agrippa answers in cold mockery, 'You think you can make me into a Christian?' This is what matters most to Paul. He wants his freedom but, more than that, he wants people to believe in Jesus.

The twist in the tale is that, had Paul not appealed to the Emperor, Festus would have been able to set him free. But to the Emperor and to Rome he must now go.

I'll bet the headlines in heaven are about someone's little kindness

Paul sails for Rome
Acts 27:1–6

When it was decided that we should sail to Italy, they handed Paul and some other prisoners over to Julius, an officer in the Roman regiment called 'The Emperor's Regiment'... Aristarchus, a Macedonian from Thessalonica, was with us. (Verses 1–2)

Two things helped to keep Paul cheerful through this dreadful and dangerous voyage. His friends, Luke, the writer of Acts, and Aristarchus, were sharing the ordeal with him. Luke also writes that the Roman officer, Julius, was kind to Paul and let him visit his fellow Christians in Sidon.

People often say that they want to be famous like pop stars or footballers. Aristarchus stayed loyal to his teacher. Julius was considerate and courteous to a prisoner. They did not think that they were doing anything special. But their behaviour was noticed by Luke, who wrote it down so that, now, millions of people have read about it. Maybe you will also do some little kindness to a friend or somebody who is in need which will make a difference that is remembered.

Hugging the coastline
Acts 27:7-12

We sailed slowly for several days and with great difficulty finally arrived off the town of Cnidus. The wind would not let us go any further in that direction, so we sailed down the sheltered side of the island of Crete, passing by Cape Salmone. (Verse 7)

Try reading this whole chapter straight through or ask someone to read it to you. Luke has written it as an exciting adventure story, a tale of a voyage and shipwreck.

The voyage began on a small ship and then transferred to a larger ship which was carrying wheat. These ships sailed regularly between Egypt and Rome and took various routes according to the winds. Luke reports that, after this, they met strong winds and lost time. This was serious because it was already the middle of October and it was too dangerous to sail after the beginning of November.

During the voyage, Paul showed his faith and his leadership. He was certain that God was with them and that everyone would survive.

Here is the shipping forecast. Gale-force winds in the Mediterranean

Caught in the storm

Acts 27:13-26

Soon a very strong wind—the one called 'North-easter'—blew down from the island. It hit the ship, and since it was impossible to keep the ship headed into the wind, we gave up trying and let it be carried along by the wind. (Verses 14–15)

My grandmother's father was a sailor. One day, she saw a line of children on the beach being given bread. She ran home to ask if she could have some too. 'That's not for you,' said her mother. 'It's for the children whose fathers have been drowned at sea.'

The sea will always be dangerous. Even today, with compasses, radar and radio to help, sailors and fishermen are still drowned. The Jewish people had a real fear of the sea and saw it as something evil as well as dangerous. Navigation was done by looking at the moon and the stars, so, in a storm like Paul and his companions experienced, they had to let the wind blow them where it wished. They could only hope that they would find dry land that they recognized, before the boat broke up.

Acts 26:1—27:26
Things to do

Storm scene

Think about Paul's little boat caught in a storm. If you like drawing, make a picture of it with big waves and dark colours. If you like music, try to play something to remind you of the crashing waves and frightened sailors. Or maybe you would rather write a short story or poem about it. Do whichever you enjoy most!

Paul breaks bread
Acts 27:27-38

Paul took some bread, gave thanks to God before them all, broke it, and began to eat. They took heart, and every one of them also ate some food.
(Verses 35–36)

The storm lasted for two whole weeks. Then, one day, the sailors' sharp ears hear the sound of waves breaking on rocks. So they take soundings. They hang a weight tied to the end of a piece of rope over the side of the boat until it touches the seabed. The water is getting shallower. They are near to land!

Paul should have been below deck, chained to the other prisoners, but here he is taking the lead again. He is certain that everyone would survive. He is equally certain that God intends him to reach Rome. As the storm begins to lessen, Luke writes that Paul took bread, gave thanks and broke it. He used Jesus' own words to emphasize that God was with them all of the time.

GOD IS WITH US

Shipwrecked!
Acts 27:39-44

*The soldiers made a plan
to kill all the prisoners, in
order to keep them from swimming ashore and
escaping. But the army officer wanted to save Paul,
so he stopped them from doing this. Instead, he
ordered all those who could swim to jump
overboard first and swim ashore; the rest were to
follow, holding on to the planks or to some broken
pieces of the ship. (Verses 42–44a)*

At my school, if you were caught chewing gum, the punishment was to clean off any gum that was stuck on desks or the floor. This was a horrible job and most children stopped chewing. It was not worth it!

It seems very brutal to read that, after the ship was wrecked, the soldiers wanted to kill the prisoners rather than risk them escaping. Roman law said that if a soldier let a prisoner escape, he would be given that prisoner's sentence. This made the soldiers look after the prisoners properly.

The hero in this part of the adventure is the army officer, or centurion. He risks losing some prisoners and ending up in jail himself to save Paul's life. We do not even know his name, but we can see how God used him to help Paul to reach Rome.

120

The natives are friendly
Acts 28:1-10

When we were safely ashore, we learnt that the island was called Malta. The natives there were very friendly to us. It had started to rain and was cold, so they lit a fire and made us all welcome.

(Verses 1–2)

A new boy joins your class. He has just arrived in England from a country where there has been a war. He doesn't speak much English and is very frightened. You can either ignore him or you can help him to settle in by seeing that he has the right things or gets to the right classroom. Even a smile is a help when you are in a strange land.

The people of Malta welcomed a group of shipwrecked sailors, looked after them and, when they left, gave them the things they needed for their voyage. They did not expect their kindness to be remembered but Luke was there and he wrote it down for us to read. The way we treat people can have an effect which is far bigger than being friendly or ignoring someone.

ROME!
He's made it!
Hooray!

Rome, at last!

Acts 28:11-15

The believers in Rome heard about us and came as far as the towns of Market of Appius and Three Inns to meet us. When Paul saw them, he thanked God and was greatly encouraged. (Verse 15)

Paul's journey has been continuously dark and dangerous. He has endured a long and dangerous voyage which ended in shipwreck. Now it is all changed. The last part of the voyage is as successful as the previous part has been disastrous. He arrives in the sunny port of Puteoli with its busy waterfront and crowded beaches, with colourful sailing boats belonging to wealthy Romans.

And so Paul reaches Rome. By this time, he is old and still a prisoner wearing chains. How will this little Jewish tent-maker stand up to the emperor of the greatest empire in the world? But the message that Paul was on his way has come ahead of him. Crowds of Christians turn out to welcome him as a great leader. How encouraged and cheered Paul must have felt!

Paul meets his fellow Israelites
Acts 28:16-20

When we arrived in Rome, Paul was allowed to live by himself with a soldier guarding him. After three days Paul called the local Jewish leaders to a meeting. (Verses 16–17a)

There are two towns in Devon where some people cannot forget that they were on different sides in the Civil War that happened three hundred years ago. It is easy to reject a whole group of people because of the behaviour of a few.

You would think that Paul would have a reason not to speak to the Jews! They had opposed him for thirty years. They had had him put in prison. They had even tried to murder him. But Paul is loyal to his background and his Jewish faith. He knows that God sent Jesus to his chosen people, the Jews, and so he always goes to the Jewish communities first. Don't forget that many Jewish people did listen to Paul's teaching and recognized that Jesus was God's Son.

I'm not listening because I'm thinking about what I'm going to say next

Acts 27:27—28:20
Things to do

Made it!

Imagine Paul being welcomed in Rome by the Christians there. He was elderly and tired, and still wearing chains, but they cheered him up and gave him gifts. It was the opposite of the storm. Draw another picture, make up some more music, or a poem, to show how different it was from the storm and shipwreck. Try to imagine the tall pine trees and the white, sun-baked road.

Toby + Trish

Made it!

I'm in the first eleven at school

I'm the twelfth man!

Let's hear what you've got to say!
Acts 28:21-24

'We would like to hear your ideas, because we know that everywhere people speak against this party to which you belong.' So they fixed a date with Paul, and a large number of them came that day to the place where Paul was staying.
(Verses 22–23a)

One of our greatest modern leaders was a man called Gandhi. He was an Indian but he grew up in South Africa at a time when people were treated differently according to the colour of their skin.

Gandhi was a small man who lived simply and wore ragged clothes. His teaching was so great that he became the founder of modern India. Even when he came to England to meet the Royal Family, he wore his tatty robes and nothing on his feet, but they welcomed and listened to him.

Paul was like that. He was a little man, chained to a soldier, but his teaching was so powerful that he could send for the Jewish leaders in Rome and they turned up to hear what he had to tell them about the kingdom of God and Jesus.

125

Open your eyes!
Acts 28:21-14

Paul concluded: 'You are to know, then, that God's message of salvation has been sent to the Gentiles. They will listen!' (Verse 28)

There are two sides to every story. Even in stories where there are good and bad people, nobody is totally good or absolutely bad. We are all like that, too.

Luke's story in the book of Acts has two sides to it. On one side it is a glorious adventure which tells how brave men like Peter and Paul took the good news about Jesus all over the known world. There is also a sad side. Peter and Paul tried again and again to make the Jews accept Jesus but they did not succeed.

Paul finishes his teaching by saying that the Holy Spirit had spoken through the prophet Isaiah. He had warned the Jews that they would not recognize Jesus. Perhaps this was also part of God's plan for making Jesus known to the whole world.

Boomerang's not all good or all bad. He's all dog

Wow! It's an amazing book of ACTion!

Luke's tribute to his friend, Paul
Acts 28:30-31

For two years Paul lived in a place he rented for himself, and there he welcomed all who came to see him. He preached about the Kingdom of God and taught about the Lord Jesus Christ, speaking with all boldness and freedom. (Verses 30–31)

Paul spent two years under house arrest, guarded by soldiers. We can be sure that many a soldier came to believe in Jesus by listening and talking with him. Paul also wrote long letters of teaching and encouragement to the Christians at Ephesus and Colossae, as well as to his friend, Philemon.

At the beginning of this book, Jesus told eleven men to tell others about him in Jerusalem, Judea, Samaria, and to the ends of the earth. Thirty years later, Peter, Paul and their companions have spread the story of Jesus throughout the known world to its captial, Rome. That is a miracle.

So we have come to the end of the Amazing Book of Acts. Luke's story closes with Paul still doing what Jesus had told him to do on the road to Damascus all those years ago, telling people about the kingdom of God—telling the world about Jesus.

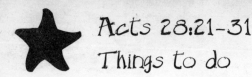

Acts 28:21-31
Things to do

Goodbye, Paul

Pretend that you are in Rome and can visit Paul in his house. What three things would you want to ask him?

Say a prayer to thank God for Paul and his friends and also for Luke, who wrote the book of Acts so that we can know all about their amazing adventures.